HOBBY LOBBY

25

26

28

30

36

38

39

40

45

46

47

48

54

56

58

Dear Friends,

Welcome! Come be our guest as we wander through a gallery of ideas for your home and ours. As we gathered some of our favorite things to share with you, we hoped that these pages would reflect the images of memories created by our mothers in days gone by.

Everyone wants to come home to a haven of comfort each day and feel the warmth of flowers, fabrics and a nice, cozy chair. Our surroundings play an important part in our lives.

As designers, we have prepared what it takes to make a "pretty picture," but through the pages ahead, we invite you to discover an inspiration of creativity for your own personal style.

Just as our mothers did, we can begin traditions of creativity when we hang that feeling of "Welcome" on our front door! We wish for you laughter and creative bursts of energy!

– Darsee Lett & Pattie Donham

Introduction

The whole world may be a stage, but for most of us, life's little dramas are played out in the comfort of our own homes, to an audience of friends and family. As the curtain rises on each new day, we find ourselves playing numerous roles, both leading and supporting, in the variety show that is our life story. We shed bitter tears of tragedy, laugh robustly through comic folly, and lose our heads and hearts to romantic dreams.

As with any other theater piece, our life drama is influenced by the details and intricacies of our surroundings. Color, texture, lighting, style...each element is critical in expressing the character we want to portray. Whether the mood is stately, sentimental or sensual, each act of living can be greatly enriched by "setting the scene".

The following pages are an invitation to discover your own personal style and artistic potential. The first section explores decorating possibilities; the second section contains a variety of spectacular projects you can make to enrich your home.

Creating Space

Everyone requires an environment of his own choosing. Before my daughter was born, I spent hours painting happy, colorful shapes on the walls in the nursery. One of the first sentences she put together was, "I don't like those things on my walls." I encouraged her to choose her own decor, and she learned at a very early age that she had some control over her life; she could participate in the creation of her own environment.

A Place for Everything and Everyone

To ensure the greatest harmony, everything and everyone needs their own space. A home is a living thing. The requirements of the whole family need to be considered. Allow your living space to come together without judgments about what you think it's supposed to look like according to an "expert". Expose yourself to a variety of choices; expand your knowledge of what is required, and pursue all the possibilities before making choices.

Make a list of the family needs: Dad needs an office, carpentry shop, garden shed; Mom needs a computer terminal, place to paint, write, sew; sister needs a place to practice dance, piano, do homework, and brother needs a place to play basketball, read, work out and spend time with a favorite hobby.

My husband and I both enjoy doing stretching exercises in the morning. Our living room offered the space we needed to feel comfortable with our morning moves. Decorating was simple. Lots of plants, pillows, decorative lamps, curtains and pictures give the room a decorated look as well as an attractive, expansive feeling. Children particularly enjoy the wide, open space. My husband and I resist the compelling urge to fill it up. Our life-style created the perfect living room for us. Comfortable couches and chairs nestled in a smaller room satisfy the need for cozy spaces where people can talk.

Developing Your Own Style

Trust your taste. Begin collecting pictures of rooms that appeal to you. Select samples from casual country to traditional classic. Don't even try to be consistent. Let your "decorating theme" emerge from an evaluation of needs and a multitude of impressions.

- Collect pictures of colors, textures, lighting techniques and fabrics.
- Cut out pictures of bathrooms, bedrooms, kitchens, living rooms, dining rooms, family rooms, alcoves and sun porches.

- Collect pictures of windows, skylights, entrance halls and gardens.

- Cut out pictures of furniture, appliances, art, anything and everything that catches your fancy...curtains, drapery, wall papers, wood work, sculpture, etc.

- Secure them in clear plastic sheets, and organize them by categories in a large three ring binder. Label the different categories with plastic tags or colored dividers. Look through your collection of favorites every day, and keep adding pictures until you feel like you have enough to represent what you like.

- Browse in your favorite stores. Try new ones. Visit museums, galleries and antique stores. Attend tours of restored homes and go to estate auctions. Visit decorator showcases in elegant mansions and historical estates. Check out model homes.

- Bring a sketch book or a camera along to make "visual notes" of things that appeal to you; a fireplace, breakfront, carpet, wall treatment, staircase, lighting fixture, the bath tub, an arboretum, traditional or non traditional rooms, exposed beams, columns, railings, ceilings. Include these in your decorating binder.

The idea is to immerse yourself in a variety of possibilities that appeal to you, allowing your personal preferences to emerge. Eventually, your decorating themes will come together. They will shape themselves into a 'look' that may surprise you and give you a good feeling about your choices. When you are trying to accommodate the needs of a living environment and introduce a style that holds it all together, it helps to be able to draw from rich, extensive research. Your decorator binder can be an invaluable source of reference. If you take the time to plan, you won't be tempted to buy bits and pieces of things that you like now, and want to change for things that look better later.

6

General Guidelines

Most people don't have the luxury of decorating without previous possessions. Rooms needing a new, fresh look can be a challenge if we don't want to give up some of our familiar arrangements or treasured things. Don't worry. There are many options for freshening up a tired room that don't involve drastic changes or a large expense.

Doing Something Different With the Windows

Creating a new window treatment can be like painting a picture or choosing just the right frame for a view that is already in place. You can emphasize it, play it down or cover it altogether. A window treatment can include shades, swags, decorative rods, lace panels, draped or tiered curtains or shutters.

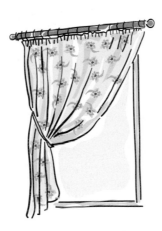

When selecting a window treatment, consider light and noise control, privacy and energy conservation. If the window is awkwardly placed or is an inappropriate shape, adding a small shade, curtain pattern that matches the walls or adding some plain draperies will de-emphasize it. If the window has a charming view and an interesting shape, an elaborate top treatment might look great.

Altering the existing window treatment can brighten a room that has gone stale. Curtains that have too much life in them to discard can be trimmed with an accent color, lace or ruffles. They can be tied back or removed altogether.

The window panes can be replaced or covered with custom designed leaded or stained glass; the window frame can be painted in different colors; vines and flowers can be stenciled around the frame, or if the view is compelling, you can leave the window bare.

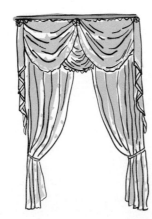

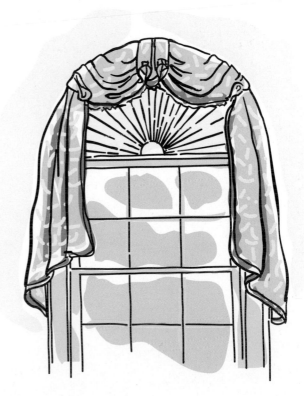

Indoor-Outdoor Living

Adding fresh or artificial greenery and floral arrangements are a relatively inexpensive way to freshen the environment and dramatically change the way a room looks and feels. Bringing the outside inside gives a natural transition, a flowing of energy that can dispel a drastic "fed up mood" and expensive wild urge to throw everyting out and redecorate from scratch.

Sometimes a house full of fresh plants can be a burden. For those fine decorators who have brown thumbs or an environment that doesn't support fresh plants, an extensive selection of economical, green and flowering artificial trees and bushes have become available in many stores throughout the country. They create the impression of an indoor garden without the inconvenience of climate control and care. Mingled with a few real plants, they take on the feeling of authentic greenery as well.

Arranged on decks that are either too sunny for most live plants to survive, or in shady areas where nothing will grow, artificial greenery is a time and water saving way to beautify your home. Place them around an austere entrance, or add them to special places throughout the house where light is scarce. Plants are often used to replace drapes or shades.

Big plants look especially good at night. Light them from below with uplights or small spots, so the light filters up through the leaves and casts patterns on the ceiling. Down lights, too, can be used to throw shafts of light down from the ceiling through the foliage.

Add twinkle lights to artificial ficus trees during the holidays and big red bows to poinsettia bushes. Blossom trees look beautiful in pastel bedrooms or next to a mural in the dining room. Combine different heights and shapes in groupings. A six-foot tree, a four-foot bush and some pots of greenery that sit on the floor will provide a natural garden look.

The containers also add to the decor. Place greenery in metal or mirrored containers, neat wooden boxes, attractive baskets, rustic pottery, or ornate ceramic containers. Indoor planter boxes can be filled with a variety of different sizes and styles of plants. Add a few silk flowers amidst the foliage for color.

Doors and Walls

Specialized paint effects have been in and out of style in response to decorating trends throughout history. The nineties offers an extensive range of techniques to beautify your doors and walls. The traditional, opaque, neutral or white shades that dominated the decorating scene for the past twenty years are becoming options instead of traditional solutions.

There are many books by experts that show you how to make a masterpiece out of a wall, door, floor or piece of furniture. One of my favorite techniques is applying layers of softly colored, see through glazes with a sponge. It is as easy to do as washing the walls, and the colors take on the look of an impressionist painting. Discreetly distressed finishes on furniture give a "lived in" highly personalized feeling. Touches of fruit sorbet colors can be added as accents or borders. Sponging, stippling, dappling and combing wall surfaces are just a few of the popular possibilities available today.

Change the look of your home by changing the style of your doors. Paint the panels and molding different colors, replace the doors with different styles or leave them off altogether. Remove the old moldings and add decorative ones. Stencils are fun and easy to do. Look for them in your local craft store or make one of your own. Remember the potato prints you made in kindergarten? Try cutting some interesting shapes out of different vegetables, dip them in acrylic paint and stamp an original border around a window or door. Practice on paper first.

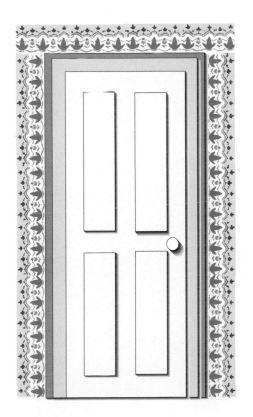
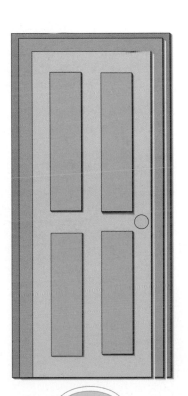
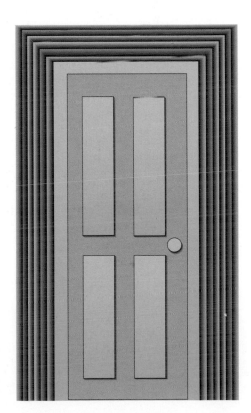

Changing the Accents

Adding some concealed up lights in corners, eye catching accent rugs, a decorative room divider, book shelves, new cushions, some nice prints, paintings or photographs, a round end table with a floor length skirt, some accent borders around the ceiling, doors and windows are just a few selective ways to give a room a decorative lift without making drastic changes.

The best time to redecorate is after you have been away for awhile. Living with things the way they are from day to day renders home decor anonymous. Coming home from a vacation lets you see your home with a fresh eye and more objectivity. It's a good time to make transformations or add a few new accents.

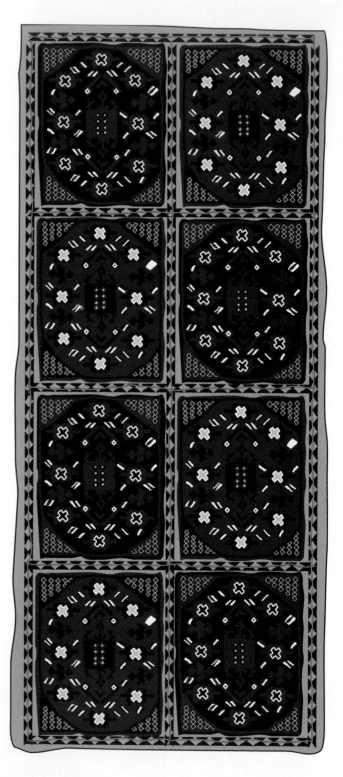

STARTING FROM SCRATCH

A Step-by-Step Overview

1. Sketch out a floor plan that includes where new furniture as well as existing furniture will be placed. Include the position of lighting fixtures, the color scheme, plants, flower arrangements, window, floor and wall treatments.

   Create a clear picture of each room in your mind's eye by putting the details down on paper. Be bold. Dare to include the things you really want. You can always align and modify your choices to fit your budget. Give yourself permission to mentally create your dream. Everything begins with an idea, a wish, a plan.

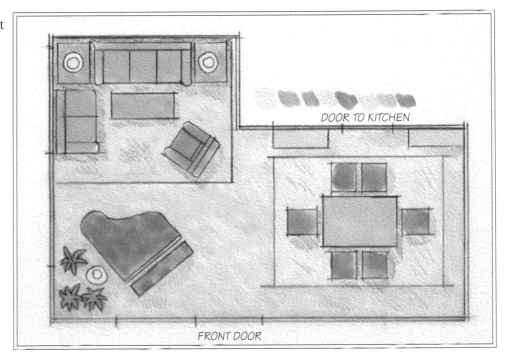

DOOR TO KITCHEN

FRONT DOOR

2. Establish a theme for each room, a style: country, Quaker simplicity, Victorian, traditional, contemporary, eclectic. This will guide you in the selection of furnishings. No matter how charming your choices, if they don't resonate a thoughtful plan, the room will appear awkward and confused.

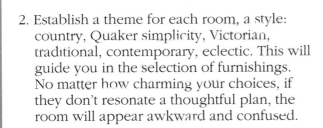

3. Every room needs a main attraction, something predominant, a focal point that you can build around: a painting, piano, four-poster bed, fireplace, or a handsome piece of furniture. When you walk into the room, something beautiful should invite you to stay.

4. Include cozy seating areas where people can snack and talk. Have furniture you can curl up in to read and dream, somewhere in your master plan. Lamps and tables accessibly placed for easy living are important features for comfort and convenience.

5. The size of the furniture should be in proportion to the size of the people in the family. The men shouldn't feel like they might break or damage furniture designed for a petite woman. Everyone needs to feel both psychologically and physically comfortable.

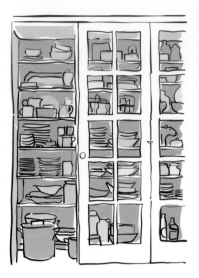

6. Leave plenty of open spaces that allow the air to move about and the room to breathe. Under utilize your space. Rooms fill up quickly with all the paraphernalia of living.

7. Create storage space for magazines, scrap books, photo albums, fine linens, china and newspapers. End tables, armoires, secretaries and coffee tables can be potential storage places to keep a room from getting a cluttered look.

8. A built-in dining room display can provide space to see and touch collectibles. Organization is determined by decorating style.

9. Strategically placed on a major kitchen wall, the kitchen pantry can hold all the family china, copper, canned and bottled goods. The kitchen pantry is the ultimate storage unit. Glass doors provide easy access and an added dimension to the wall

10. Avoid the "furniture store look" where a sterile, stage set living or dining room repels the life and energy of the family as well as friends and guests. Each room should reveal the intimacy of private lives lived un-self-consciously and comfortably.

11. Odd spaces make the most unique decorating problems. A cozy escape with a view from a balcony overlooking the living room provides the perfect spot to read or reflect. With natural light and an open airy space for family and friends, a secluded area can have all the requisites for a small library or a big snooze.

12. Painted screens provide a beautiful backdrop for a table used as a stage for showing off arrangements. They can hide a rack of off season clothing, or fill and decorate an awkward corner.

13. Well-lit rooms enliven and invite us to participate in the possibilities and comfort of our home. Light candles. Install dimmer switches to control the brightness of overhead lights. Highlight paintings and install indirect lighting on shelves and around cornices. Put lamps on tables for reading, and have standing lamps reflecting soft lights for a cozy feeling.

14. The transition between inside and outside can be easy and natural when plants and flowers surround and adorn the furnishings. Clean windows carry us outside at a glance. Organic wall papers and blues, greens, yellows...colors found in nature remind us of natural beauty and help us to feel at home in our home.

15. Let your mind flow from one thing to another. Avoid obvious matching of chairs to furniture, drapes to bedspreads, head boards to high boys. Subtle differences between patterns and styles are interesting to look at and wear well.

16. Avoid the clutter of too many knick knacks and travel mementos. Dolls and stuffed animals are more appropriate in the bedroom than the living room, and collections of tea cups, jade or figurines should be displayed at special times and not part of your

everyday experience. Accumulated "objects" burden a room and occupy space that could be open to something new and fresh.

17. Experiment! Combine antique pieces that you love with traditional or contemporary settings. Antiques are a good investment. The more beautiful they are, the more their value increases over the years. Add touches of vivid colors that make you feel good. Use a drawing table for a desk, a steamer trunk for a coffee table, baskets to hold everyday clutter and unmatched sofa end tables. Organize and reorganize; combine and recombine. Your home is a living experience. it is a refuge of energy and renewal.

Well organized storage space is essential to comfortable living. The more apparel that can be tucked away in an orderly fashion, the greater the feeling of space you can create. Whether you have built in closets or free standing storage systems improvised with screens or curtains, the arrangement of stored items requires planning.

Make a list of categories, and group similar items together. Use combinations of shelves, containers, drawers and hooks for every category. Build shelves above the rod to store things you don't use every day, like: luggage and linens. Walls can support hooks for ties, belts, hats and scarves. Shoes take up a lot of room. If space is tight, hang a shoe bag on the back of a door, or put shoe racks on shelves or on the floor. If you store your shoes in boxes, label the fronts so you know which shoes are in which box.

Only part of your wardrobe may need to be hung in the closet. Create a place somewhere else for out of season clothing, accessories and shoes. Portable garment racks, baskets and containers can be tucked away in an alcove behind a painted screen. Stuff can be stored in a cedar chest at the foot of your bed or in a curtained off corner of your room.

Shoe boxes are great for keeping things neat. Use them to separate socks from tights. They will usually fit in a standard size, dresser drawer. Cover some boxes with wall paper, fill them up with accessories, and stack them on a dresser. They can add to the decor.

Young children need lots of storage space for toys, clothing and books. A well ordered play room makes it easy for a child to put away his own belongings. Improvise storage in brightly colored boxes and on shelves. Use space under beds by propping the bed up on cube storage units. Stacking units are great for toys while children are young, and can be used for other things as your child grows.

Louvered doors allow air to circulate and keep clothes from smelling musty. Scented candles, cedar balls, sachets, or an open empty perfume bottle will also add to your closet aesthetics. Initially it may take time to organize and plan your storage spaces, but the added space and feeling of orderliness is worth it.

Everyone has a personal color preference, a combination of colors they find most pleasing. They are called 'subjective colors'. Identifying and using our subjective colors does more than make our environment attractive. It helps us to connect with ourselves; It is therapeutic.

Colors radiate qualities of energy that affect us positively or negatively, whether we are aware of it or not. Colors do not have to be colorful to have an emotional effect. Some people are drawn to muted shades, just as other people are drawn to a brighter palette. If you are drawn to one color, say blue in your clothing and furnishing, you tend to see other colors in relation to blue.

Colors are one of the most important choices you will need to make when decorating a room. By coordinating colors, patterns and textures, you can provide a harmonious, enlivening and pleasing place. What combinations make you feel relaxed, excited, uncomfortable. Do you enjoy pale or vivid colors?

Begin planning your color scheme by noticing the colors around you, wherever you are. Look out the window and notice the color of the sky next to the various shades of green in the landscape or the red tiled roof. The next time you go to the beach, look at the beige color of the sand against the blue sky and white clouds; the sand dunes covered with purple sage, the emerald green and blue/gray ocean edged with white foam meeting the slate gray, wet rocks. Nature delivers up the most beautiful and restful combinations of colors. All we have to do is notice them, really see them. To have an impression of the overall coloring of a scene, try closing your eyes half way. The details will fade away leaving you with a sense of the color relationships.

Fail Safe Rooms

Neutral rooms

Nature's pallette provides an abundant variety of neutral shades. Create a background of earthy tones that make you feel like you are moving through softly colored rain clouds. The subtle tones and textures suggest a wide range of accents. Once you have set the scene, change the room by adding new attractions.

Off-whites, putty, beige, grays, sepias, tobacco and slate colors all blend easily in a room. They provide a great background for pictures, flowers and furniture. Calming and cool, neutral colors can look drab if they are not combined with interesting textures: stone and wood, marble, lacquer, silk, satin, velvet and matting are perfect remedies for a drab neutral environment. Dull reds, shiny blacks, mauves, pinks or yellow-greens make beautiful, contrasting colors in a neutral room.

White Plus One Color

Shades of white for as far as the eye can see, accented with pale blue, slate gray, brick pink or violet gray can look very elegant and be very versatile. Brilliant white is hard to live with, but off whites feel very restful to most people. If you enjoy change, it is easy to alter the look of a white room by adding different colors and textures as accents. A room decorated in shades of off-white, lends itself to all styles: lace curtains, a brass bed and wicker furniture; wide shutters on the windows, giant banana leaves and a wrought iron canopy bed; or a white lacquer sofa, billowing drapes and a rattan gliding rocker.

Monochromatic Rooms

Monochromatic rooms are very popular and easy to create. Combinations of shades, tints and tones of one color, the monochromatic decorating scheme gives a very rich and subtle feeling. Fabrics are usually solid shades or quiet, tone on tones and are softly textured. Large patterns, stripes and florals usually don't work. Avoid dramatic fabric statements. They detract from the flow of texture and color. The upholstery in all of the seating is usually the same. Textures are supple and sumptuous: nubby wools, buttery leathers, velours and cottons.

Relieve the monotony of the ongoing color with major artwork, huge, live or artificial plants, contrasting dull and shiny textures like a plush mat carpet and a gleaming glass coffee table. Small doses of complementary colors will also keep the room lively. Monochromatic rooms have a comfortable, coordinated look. Everything blends together.

Lots of indirect lighting behind standing plants, over pictures, in corners or around the ceiling will add to the charm and cozy feeling of the similar colors. Add table lamps for comfortable reading places. Libraries, television rooms or any room where the activity is more introverted or passive, correspond well with monochromatic decor.

Grayed-down Shades and Tones

Grayed-down colors, shades and tones look fabulous together. Rich rusts, ochres, olive greens and deep violets create a nostalgic effect. Delight the senses with subtle patterns, stripes and solids. Use the colors from a dried flower arrangement or a package of potpourri. Add some drab green or dark maroon for tonal contrast and strength. Grayed-down colors give an aged impression. They look great with painted furniture that is slightly distressed. The floors can be highly polished, stained or painted with a dull glaze. Rag rugs or oriental carpets also add to the richness of the color scheme.

Study what effect light has at different times of the day. Does your room need touches of shiny, hard textures like pewter, crystal or black lacquer. Would a big palm tree, some cactus or hanging ferns add to that final touch. How about clusters of baskets to hold odds and ends like newspapers, knitting projects or magazines.

Other Sources of Inspiration

Use a piece of fabric with a pleasing color combination to coordinate the colors in a room. Build a room around the colors in a color print or painting. An eye catching area rug can provide your color scheme. Create a unified feeling in the room by using the colors in the rug on pillows and in floral accents.

Raw Color

The color wheel divides colors into warm and cool: red, orange and yellow: blue green and violet. Warm colors come to meet you and cool colors shy away. Warm colors require less light to be seen and cool colors come alive when they are in the spot light.

The full intensity of a color is called a "hue". A "tint" is a hue lightened with white. A "tone" is a hue mixed with gray, and a "shade" is a hue darkened with black.

Red, blue and yellow are the primary colors. Mix equal amounts of these colors together, and you have secondary colors: orange, green and purple. Yellow and blue make green, red and yellow make orange and blue and red make purple. Mix various amounts of black or white to primary or secondary colors, and you have the full spectrum of colors, shades and tones.

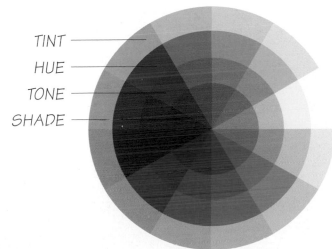

TINT

HUE

TONE

SHADE

Monochromatic colors are shades of one color like: pink, rose, mauve and burgundy. The energy is subtle and soothing.

Analogous colors are colors that are next to each other on the color wheel. They include one primary color and at least one fourth of the color wheel. Yellow, yellow-orange, orange and red-orange blend to create a popular color harmony for a warm, cozy feeling.

Complementary colors are opposite one another on the color wheel. Violets and yellows and peaches and greens create a vivid contrast. They have an enlivening effect on each other. Complementary colors are lively, crisp and exciting.

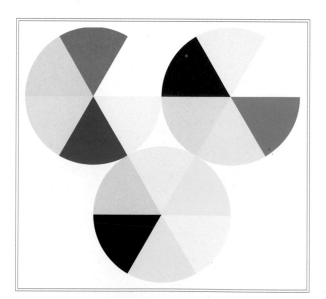

A triad of colors consists of any three colors equally spaced that fall at the points of a triangle placed anywhere on the color wheel. Red, yellow, blue; or orange, green and violet can be used as accents in a neutral room or combined to create a balanced, vivid harmony of colors.

Decorative Accents

Like cherries on the top of ice cream sundaes, decorative accents provide the finishing touch to a dining table, entrance hall, bedside table, wall, desk or coffee table. They reflect your personality, creativity and inner feelings, especially if you have made them yourself. They can add just the right color, shape and texture to freshen a too familiar surrounding.

Start with things you love: a special container, your favorite flowers, driftwood or found objects. Your project or arrangement doesn't have to be perfect. Your intention and creative energy pouring into your home will benefit and inspire family members and guests.

Houses require love, attention and appreciation in order for them to evolve into gracious, living environments. Decorating is a life time career; the art of placement a time honored tradition. So, whether you are starting fresh or adding to something in progress, plan your dream, and enjoy working your plan.

Part 2

Home
Accents

RAFFIA BOW

1 Cross raffia ends making the tails as long as you want. Where the raffia crosses is the center of the bow.

2 Bring the center together with the crossed raffia, and secure it with a small wire.

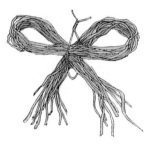

3 Take a few strands of raffia and wrap it around the center of the bow to hide the wire. Hot glue the ends together in the back.

4 To attach extra tails, cut a length of raffia that is long enough for both tails. Wrap the center of the raffia around the wired center, and either wire the tails together in the back or hot glue them to secure.

Variations of the raffia bow: Add extra tails, stagger the length of the tails, exaggerate the diameter of the center of the bow or add the tails after you have made the basic bow.

FLORIST BOW

These directions describe how to make a bow using three yards of ribbon. By adjusting the streamer length, loop size and number of loops, the same technique can be used to make any size bow.

1 Measure about 14" for the first tail. With the right side of the ribbon facing out, make a loop on one side using 8-9" of ribbon. Pinch the ribbon together, and hold it with your thumb and forefinger.

2 Twist the ribbon so the right side is facing out, and make a loop toward the other side.

3 Repeat the process of twisting the ribbon as you continue to make loops on both sides. Make each set of loops a little smaller than the previous set.

4 To complete the bow, twist the remaining ribbon around your thumb to make the center loop. Adjust the tail so the right side is facing out. Put a piece of wire through the center and twist it at the back of the bow. The wire should be tight enough to secure the bow, but loose enough to adjust the loops.

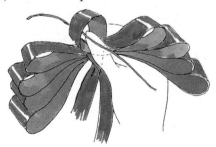

5 Spread the loops of the bow, and cut the ends of the tails.

LOOPY BOW

1 Make a loop leaving the tail the desired length.

2 Continue making loops, keeping them uniform in size, until the bow is full, and you have enough ribbon left over to make the remaining tail.

3 Secure the center of the bow with floral wire.

4 Fan out the loops

5 Cut the tails at an angle or in points to finish off the bow.

TAILORED BOW

Double Sided Ribbon

1 Fold ribbon as shown, decreasing loop size on each layer.

2 Staple all the layers together.

3 Add a length of ribbon behind loops (two tails) and staple underneath loops.

4 Wrap a length of ribbon around center of bow and glue ends together in back.

Single Sided Ribbon

1 Cut 3 different lengths of ribbon. Overlap ends 1", and staple centers.

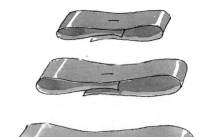

2 Stack loops and staple all thicknesses together.

3 Wrap a length of ribbon around center of bow, and glue ends together in back.

4 Optional tail: glue pointed tails to back of center loop.

Plantation Prelude

Materials

- 11 Yds. (gold) mesh ribbon
- 6 Yds. (gold) cording
- Florist wire
- Gold spray paint

Silk flowers

- 12 Stems magnolia foliage
- 10 Stems (white) dogwood
- 3 Bunches plumosus fern
- 6 Stems magnolias, large
- 2 Garlands (green) English ivy
- 2 Garlands (variegated) English ivy

Tools

- Wire cutters
- Scissors
- Hot or low melt glue gun/glue sticks

Suggested substitutions:
Ficus leaves for magnolia foliage
Cosmos for dogwood
Maidenhair fern for plumosus
Roses for magnolias
Any kind of greenery garlands for ivy

Instructions

1 Green ivy. Spray ivy gold, and allow to dry.

2 Magnolia foliage and hanging loops. Wire the branches together, forming a square at the top in proportion to a door frame. Make hanging loops at the corners and in the center.

3 Gold and variegated ivy. Wind the gold garlands throughout the magnolia leaves, starting at the middle of the wired magnolia branches. Repeat using the variegated ivy.

4 Ribbon. Cut four yards of ribbon, and make a 10" wide loopy bow with 12" tails (see page 21). Wire the bow to the top center of the garland.

5 Remaining ribbon. Cut in half and glue ends under the ribbon loops on each side of the bow. Drape down each side of the garland, alternating from side to side, securing with glue gun as you go. Allow 8" on each side to dangle from the ends of the garland.

6 Magnolias. Cut blooms from stems. Glue two into the loops of the bow and two on each side where the garland bends.

7 Gold cording. Cut the cording in half. Secure the ends with knots, and glue one on each side of the loopy bow. Wind in and around the leaves, draping and alternating directions, gluing as you go. Allow a few inches to dangle from the ends.

8 Dogwood and plumosus. Scatter individual flowers throughout the garland. Distribute the fern throughout. Glue to secure.

Project is 56" tall and 56" wide.

Note: Instructions for the "Angelic Door Swag" are on page 24.

Angelic Door Swag

Materials

- 9" to 10" Long papier-mache cherub
- 2 Yds. (gold) cording
- Florist wire
- Gold spray paint

Silk flowers

- 1 Garland (variegated) English ivy
- 1 Garland (green) English ivy
- 2 Bunches preserved plumosus fern
- 3 Stems magnolia foliage
- 3 Stems (ivory) magnolias, large
- 2 Stems dogwood

Tools

- Wire cutters
- Hot or low melt glue gun/glue sticks

Suggested substitutions:
Holland ivy for variegated ivy
Begonia leaves for green ivy
Maidenhair for plumosus
Hydrangea leaves for magnolia leaves
Roses for magnolias
Cosmos for dogwood

Instructions

1 Cherub and green ivy. Spray the cherub and green English ivy garland with gold paint. Allow to dry.

2 Gold cherub and hanging loop. Make a hanging loop on the back of the gold cherub using floral wire.

3 Magnolia foliage and cherub. Attach foliage into the hanging loop of the cherub using wire.

4 Gold ivy. Wind gold ivy garland through the magnolia branches. Secure with glue gun.

5 Variegated ivy. Wind variegated ivy garland through the branches. Secure with glue gun.

6 Magnolias. Cut the stems from three magnolias and glue to foliage. (See photo for placement.)

7 Dogwood. Pull the blooms from the dogwood stems, and glue throughout swag.

Secret: Combine with the "Magnificent Magnolia Garland" on page 22 for an incredibly festive celebration.

8 Gold cording. Tie knots 6" from the ends. Drape the cording throughout and behind the angel and glue in place.

9 Plumosus fern. Glue sprays of plumosus fern throughout swag.

Project is 45" tall.

INTERMEZZO PLANTER

Materials

- *16" Tall plaster wall planter*
- *Floral foam*
- *Spanish moss*
- *"Rub N' Buff"™ (gold) paint*
- *Spray paint, acrylic (white)*
- *Floral pins*

Silk Greens

- *2 Sprays bear grass*
- *1 Boston fern*
- *1 Bush begonia leaf greenery*
- *1 Spray cordyline leaf foliage*
- *1 Bush ruffled fern*

Tools

- *Hot or low melt glue gun/glue sticks*
- *Serrated knife to cut foam*

Suggested substitutions:
Large pothos for Boston fern
Split leaf philo for cordyline
Polyscias bush for begonia leaf
Maple ivy for ruffled fern
Ivy for bear grass

Instructions

1 Paint. Spray paint the planter white, and highlight it with gold "Rub N' Buff".

2 Foam and moss. Cut foam to fit snugly inside planter. Hot glue to secure. Cover with moss, and secure moss with floral pins.

3 Boston and ruffled fern. Cut the stems from both bushes and insert into foam.

Secret: The best thing about this beautiful wall decoration is that you don't have to remember to water it. Place it by the pool, in the sunroom or let it be a greeting as you enter your home.

4 Begonia bush and cordyline leaf foliage. Insert begonia bush, then add cordyline leaf foliage.

5 Bear grass. Tuck bear grass sprays in front under cordyline foliage.

Project is 30" tall!

NATURAL WONDER

Materials

- 12" Tall round vase
- 1 Everlasting Elegance™ liquid glass kit

Silk flowers

- 1 Stem grape ivy leaves
- 1 Stem (orange) day lilies
- 3 Stems (purple) statice
- 1 Stem (yellow) astible orchid
- 1 Stem latex grape leaf spray
- 6 Stems plumosus fern
- 2-3 Curly willow branches 30-35" long

Tools

- Wire cutters
- Florist waterproof tape ½" wide

Suggested substitutions:
Mini nephthytis for grape ivy
Empress lilies for day lilies
Mini dasies for statice
Micro roses for orchids
Mini creeping Charlie for grape leaf
Tree fern for plumosus

Secret: There's nothing like a beautiful arrangement of silk and dried flowers to brighten a corner or give an entrance way a great first impression.

Instructions

1. Liquid glass. Pour resin into vase, according to mfg. directions.

2. Florist tape. Make a grid across the top of the vase.

3. Greenery. Insert greenery through the grid.

4. Lily and orchid. Add lily and orchid for height.

5. Statice. Fill in arrangement with statice.

6. Curly willow branches. Accent with curly willow.

7. Final touches. Place on level surface overnight for resin to set. Pull off tape when thoroughly dry.

Arrangement is approximately 30" tall

GARLAND ELEGANCE

Materials

- 5 Yds. 2" wide (burgundy rose) wire edge ribbon
- 1 Oz. Spanish and deerfoot moss
- Florist wire
- 20 Dried orange slices
- 15 Dried apple slices
- 5 Large berry clusters

Silk and dried flowers

- 8 Stems (pink) open roses
- 6 Stems (pink) rose buds
- 9 Stems (burgundy) open roses
- 3 Garlands English ivy
- 6 Stems (natural) caspia
- 6 Stems (purple) statice (or artemesia)

Tools

- Florist wire
- Wire cutters
- Hot or low melt glue gun/glue sticks

Suggested substitutions:
Peonies for roses
Tweedia for rosebuds
Mini Holland ivy for English ivy
Baby's breath for caspia
Freesias for statice

Project is 86" long

Instructions

1 Ivy garlands. Weave the garlands together, and secure with florist wire.

2 All roses and buds. Cut stems to 2" long, and hot glue in a random fashion on three sides of the garland.

3 Caspia. Wire small bunches together, and wire or hot glue into leaves.

4 Statice. Cut individual clusters leaving 1" stems. Hot glue throughout garland.

5 Various mosses. Mix small clumps together, and glue into leaves to soften and fill in garland.

6 Dried apple and orange slices. Distribute throughout, gluing to secure.

7 Berry clusters. Equally space the berry clusters along the garland.

8 Ribbon. Tie the ribbon at one end, and wind it around the garland, pushing it into and around the leaves. Tie it off at the other end.

Secret: Adorn a curving window, edge a vanity table, wrap this luscious garland around a favorite wall hanging, drape it casually over a standing screen or lay it across a mantelpiece, hugging the bases of the candlesticks.

FOREST RHAPSODY

Materials

- 1 Garland English ivy
- 2 Dried pomegranates, medium
- 3 Dried pomegranates, large
- 2 Decorative birds
- 3 Crab apple sprays
- 12 Dried apple slices
- Forest lichen
- Small amounts of sphagnum, deerfoot and Spanish moss
- Florist wire

Dried flowers

- 6 Stems (navy) sorrell
- 6 Stems (burgundy) sorrell
- 6 Stems statice, artemesia or natural sago-smokebush

Tools

- Scissors
- Hot or low melt glue gun/glue sticks

Suggested substitutions:
Gyp for sorrell
Pepper grass for statice

Optional: Birdcage is 30" tall. Garland may also be used for other sizes and shapes of cages as well as on a mantlepiece or over a doorway.

Instructions

1 Forest lichen, garland and mosses. Wire or hot glue clusters of lichen and mosses into garland.

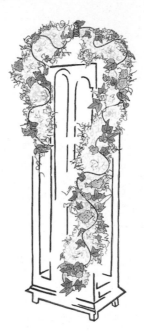

2 Pomegranates, crab apples and apple slices. Arrange throughout garland, and hot glue to secure.

3 Dried flowers. Break into 4" pieces, wire small mixed bunches together, and glue throughout, into garland.

4 Birds. Wire garland to birdcage, and glue on birds.

Garland is 72" long.

Secret: To create a charming, wooden birdcage base for your garland, spray birdcage with acrylic, burgundy spray paint. Allow to dry. Spread navy blue acrylic paint with a sponge in a few areas. Wipe with a cloth. Brush on some gold paint in a few areas, and wipe with cloth again; let dry. Use steel wool for a distressed effect.

31

Materials

- *2 Yds (white) tulle ribbon*
- *3 Yds. (white) 36" wide, lace fabric*
- *Florist wire*

Silk flowers

- *3 Garlands (variegated) ivy*
- *4 Stems (white) gypsophila*
- *2 Stems (white) tiger lily (2 flowers, 1 bud each)*
- *4 Stems (white) statice*

Tools

- *Scissors*

Suggested substitutions:
English ivy for variegated ivy
Field flowers for gypsophila
Day lilies for tiger lilies
Freesia for statice

Instructions

1 Ivy garlands and hanging loops. Lay garlands, side by side. Wire them together at the corners of the window (or picture, etc.). Make hanging loops from florist wire.

2 Day lily, gypsophila and statice. Gather a bouquet of half the flowers in your hand, and attach to a corner using florist wire. Repeat for the other corner.

3 Fabric. Lay fabric on a table and place the garland on top to establish the corners.

4 Tulle ribbon. Cut the ribbon in half. Tie the fabric, flowers and garland together, at the corners, with the tulle ribbon. Top the corners with tulle bows.

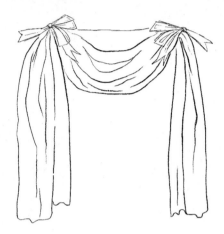

Secret: An easy, no sew method for curtains on any small window. Try one of Grannie's old, lace tablecloths, or look for interesting lace remnants at garage sales.

TEA TIME WREATH

Materials

- 18" Grapevine wreath
- 1 Pair (pink) gloves
- 1 Teacup and saucer
- 1 Plate hanger
- 4 Yds. (ivory) wire edged, fancy ribbon
- ⅓ Yd. (ivory) ½" satin ribbon
- Florist wire

Silk flowers

- 5 Stems (pink) cabbage roses
- 3 Stems (pink) rose buds
- 5 Stems (ivory) cabbage roses
- 3 Sprays (ivory) micro roses (5 flowers each)

Note: Substitute peonies for roses and tweedia for rose buds if materials are not available.

Dried flowers

- Small amounts of each: Plumosus fern, (green & purple) statice, caspia, salal leaves, or any other similar dried materials.

Tools

- Scissors
- Wire cutters
- Hot or low melt glue gun/glue sticks

Instructions

1 Saucer, plate hanger, hanging loop. Glue saucer in plate hanger. Secure to wreath with wire. Make hanging loop.

2 Ribbon. Cut ribbon in half. Glue one piece to top of wreath, and wrap all the way around. Make a 7" wide loopy bow with the remaining ribbon. (See page 21.) Secure the bow with wire to the top of the wreath.

3 Cup and gloves, ribbon. Tie the ½"ribbon around cup handle and cuff of gloves. Glue underneath bow loops.

4 Pink and white large roses and buds. Cut the stems to 2" long, and glue to wreath (see photo).

5 Micro roses. Cut into five bunches, and glue onto wreath.

6 Salal leaves. Tuck or glue the leaves throughout the wreath.

7 Small amount of dried material. Glue small amounts throughout the wreath.

Secret: You can hang any object from the center of the wreath: an old violin, reading glasses, a vintage christening gown...anything that looks good or is meaningful to you.

Nature's Palette
(A Decorating Technique)

Materials

- Straight sided natural basket
- Papier mache oval box with lid.
- Aleene's tacky glue™

Dried flowers

(Note: Any dried materials may be used.)

- (Pink) tea rosebuds
- (Burgundy) preserved wild yarrow
- Preserved eucalyptus leaves
- (Purple) poa/phalaris
- (Yellow) natural achillea yarrow
- Forest lichen
- (Green) sheet moss

Tools

- Scissors

Note: This technique can be used on wooden boxes, baskets or any Styrofoam based projects.

Secret: Use that sentimental, dried corsage lovingly placed in your bottom drawer. Nestle it among the dried rosebuds and other materials to create a decorative memory.

Instructions

1 Dried material. Snip off the tops of all the dried material. Remove the leaves from the eucalyptus.

2 Tacky glue. Liberally spread glue on project base. Glue drieds onto basket or paper box in layers. Use contrasting colors next to each other.

3 Sheet moss and lichen. Fill in open areas with moss and lichen.

Natural Harvest

Materials

- 14" Preserved eucalyptus wreath
- Floral wire

Dried flowers

(Note: Any dried materials may be used. Select interesting colors and textures)

- 5 Sprays (white) Australian daisies
- 3 Bunches natural safflower
- 9 Stems (purple) papaver/poppy pods
- 3 Bunches (green) sage
- 2 Bunches (tan) natural lepidium
- 1 Bunch (white) ti tree

Tools

- Hot or low melt glue gun/glue sticks
- Scissors

Secret: Use the wreath as a centerpiece, hugging an oil lamp or a hurricane shade with a candle inside.

Instructions

1 All dried materials. Cut stems to 2" long. Wire small clusters of similar material together. Leave poppy pods and safflowers aside.

2 Wires. Glue or wire clusters to wreath in a circular pattern.

3 Poppy pods & safflowers. Cut stems to 2" long, and glue clusters in-between dried materials.

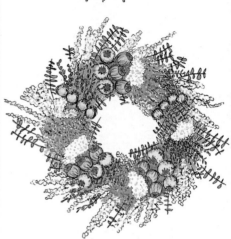

Materials

- *3" Floral foam balls*
- *Aleene's tacky glue™*

Dried flowers

Note: Any dried materials may be used.

- *Poppy pods, natural or dyed*
- *Safflowers or carthamus*
- *Nigella orientalis, natural or dyed*
- *Salignum or pine cones*
- *Mountain flowers or jazildas*

Tools

- *Paint brush*
- *Paper plate*
- *Scissors*

Instructions

1 Dried materials. Snip the heads off, leaving ¾ " stems to insert into foam.

2 Tacky glue. Pour glue onto paper plate. Cover ⅓ of the foam ball with glue.

3 Flower heads. Push flower heads into glue-coated foam. Place them close together. Continue process until ball is covered.

Secret: Sprinkle with potpourri oil for subtle fragrance.

ENGLISH GARDEN IN A POT

Materials

- 12" Wide X 10" tall clay pot
- 2 Floral foam (enough to fill the pot)
- 2 Wire wreath forms 15"
- 4 Wooden floral stakes, 6" long
- Florist wire
- Spanish moss
- Floral pins

Silk flowers

- 1 Silk cabbage
- 1 Bush (red) geraniums (3 flowers)
- 1 Spray feaverview
- 2 Stems wild mini daisies
- 1 Stem (orange) black-eyed Susan
- 1 Bush springerii fern
- 1 Spray dusty miller
- 2 Stems (yellow) marigolds (2 flowers each)
- 2 Garlands miniature roses (orange)
- 2 Stems bulb foliage
- 5-6 Assorted twigs

Tools

- Hot or low melt glue gun/glue sticks
- Wire cutters

Note: If materials are not available, substitute with similar flowers and greenery.

Instructions

1 Pot, floral foam and moss. Fill the pot with foam, cover it with moss, and secure the moss with floral pins.

2 Wire wreath forms and floral stakes. Wire the wreaths back to back. Secure the wreaths in the back of the pot with the floral stakes.

3 Spanish moss and garlands. Push pieces of moss into wreaths. Wind one garland around wreaths. Cut the other one into 6" pieces. Set aside.

4 Bulbs, springerii, feaverview, pieces of mini rose, cabbage. Insert greenery. Glue pieces of garland into the greenery.

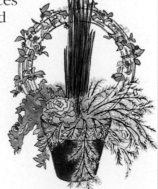

5 Geranium bush, black-eyed Susan spray, marigolds, dusty miller spray and mini daisies. Insert as shown.

6 Twigs. Scatter twigs throughout the arrangement for a natural effect.

Project is 34" tall.

Secret: Place this "little garden in a pot" where you can't get anything to grow: a balcony, rooftop, deck, under the oak trees…

FARMER'S DELIGHT

Materials

- Children's gardening tools (3 small shovels, 2 trowels)
- 2 Miniature clay pots 2 1/2" wide
- 1 Pair gardening gloves
- Various silk fruits & vegetables of your choice
- 5 Seed packets
- Florist wire
- Spanish moss
- 20 Strands of raffia

Silk flowers

- 2 Garlands pothos ivy, 6' long each
- 3 Sprays (white) baby's breath

Tools

- Hot or low melt glue gun/glue sticks
- Wire clippers

Secret: Hang your indoor harvest around the window over the kitchen sink, or around a mirror in the dining area.

Instructions

1. Pothos garlands. Weave the two garlands together, and secure with pieces of florist wire.

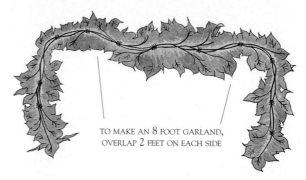

TO MAKE AN 8 FOOT GARLAND, OVERLAP 2 FEET ON EACH SIDE

2. Fruits, veggies, seed packets, gloves and garden tools. Using hot glue or florist wire, attach each to garland.

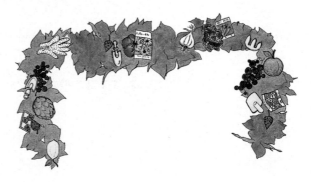

3. Baby's breath. Cut sprays into 4" pieces, and hot glue into garland.

4. Clay pots and moss. Feed florist wire through the drain hole, and secure around garland. Glue moss to inside of pots. Glue clumps of moss along garland to fill in empty places.

5. Raffia. Weave the strips of raffia throughout garland, allowing pieces to trail from the ends.

Project is approximately 8' long.

MOSS CRAZY

Materials

- 18" Heart shaped shelf with shaker peg
- 2 Pkgs. Sheet moss
- Aleene's tacky glue™
- Disposable brush
- Paper plate
- 1 Yd. (burgundy) wired ribbon
- 1 Victorian charm (gold)

Dried flowers

- 16 Stems (pink) rosebuds
- 1 Stem (white) statice

Tools

- Hot or low melt glue gun/glue sticks
- Scissors

Suggested substitutions:
Red rosebuds for pink rosebuds
Caspia for statice

Instructions

1 Tacky glue. Pour glue into paper plate, and apply to the shelf in sections with a brush.

2 Moss. Press moss onto shelf as you glue until the entire piece is covered. Allow to dry.

3 Ribbon. Using 2/3 yds., tie a simple bow, 6" wide, with 6" tails. Glue to right side of shelf. Glue remaining 12" across shelf, looping as you go. Glue bow tails to shelf.

4 Rosebuds, statice and charm. Glue clusters of roses to center of bow and down tails. Glue charm near bow. Break statice into 2-3" pieces and glue in random pattern.

Secret: Add your favorite figure sitting on the moss.

CATCH A FALLING STAR

Materials

- 8" Urethane foam star
- 3 Large (gold) charms
- 3 Small (gold) charms
- 3 Star (gold) charms
- 1 Cupid (gold) charm
- 2 Pkg. sheet moss
- Floral pins
- Aleene's tacky glue™
- Disposable brush
- Paper plate
- 1 Yd. (burgundy) cording (for hanging)
- 1 Yd. (burgundy) decorative braiding
- 1 Yd. (burgundy) 1" wired ribbon

Dried flowers

- 24 Stems (pink or red) rosebuds
- 12 Rose leaves (silk)
- 1 Stem (white) statice or caspia

Secret: Hang your star from the bedpost! To freshen sheet moss, mist it lightly with a spritz of water.

Instructions

1 Tacky glue, star and moss. Pour glue into paper plate, and apply to star in sections with a brush. Press moss into glue as you go until star is completely covered. Allow to dry.

2 Decorative braiding. Wrap around the star, tying where you begin and end. (See photo.)

3 Charms. Secure to star with floral pins or glue. Allow to dangle.

4 Ribbon. Cut ribbon in half, and make two ribbon roses. Hot glue to star.

5 Tea roses, statice and leaves. Randomly glue roses and leaves to star. Break statice into 2-3" pieces. Glue throughout.

6 Cording. Tie ends of cording to "arms" of star. Glue loose ends around the knot for a smooth finish. Hang at an angle.

Earthy Heart Box

Materials

- 9" Papier mache heart shaped box with lid
- 1 Yd (burgundy) decorative cording
- Aleene's tacky glue™
- 2 (Gold) charms
- 1 Yd (burgundy) wired ribbon
- 2 Pkgs. sheet moss
- Disposable brush and paper plate
- Floral pins

Dried flowers

- 16 Stems (pink or red) tea roses
- 1 Stem (white) statice or caspia

Tools

- Hot or low melt glue gun/glue sticks
- Scissors

Secret: Cloaked in a warm blanket of soft moss, this charming heart is a perfect place for love letters and timeless treasures. Line the inside with burgundy satin or velvet before decorating the outside of the box.

Instructions

1 Tacky glue, box and moss. Pour glue into paper plate. Apply to box in sections with brush, and press moss into glue until box is completely covered. Allow to dry.

2 Ribbon. Tie a simple bow with long tails. Glue to top of box. Glue down tails.

3 Decorative braiding. Glue loops of braiding in a random pattern.

4 Charms. Use hot glue to secure the charms.

5 Roses and statice. Cut off the stems of the roses and glue in a random pattern. Break the statice into 2-3" pieces and glue throughout.

Winter Wonderland

Materials

- 30" Pine wreath
- 5 Yds. (purple) wired ribbon
- 6 Yds. (white) tulle ribbon
- 10 Yds. (gold) 1/4" cording
- 24 Acrylic jewelry charms
- Florist wire

Tools

- Scissors

Instructions

1. **Wreath.** Fluff up the wreath

2. **Purple ribbon.** Make an 8" wide florist bow with 20" and 18" tails. (See page 20.) Secure bow to wreath with florist wire.

3. **Gold cording and charms.** Cut twenty four 12" pieces of cording. Tie to charms and hang on pine fronds.

4. **Tulle ribbon.** Cut 12" lengths and tuck into wreath fronds to soften and fill.

Secret: This wreath can hang over the fireplace or in the entrance way. For the spoon collector, this is a great way to share your treasured heirlooms. Hang candy treats and some small silver scissors to inspire guests to snip their favorite candy as a holiday treat.

Photo by Mitchell Geller

Materials

- 4" Floral foam balls
- 4" X 3" X 9" Floral foam bricks
- Aleene's tacky glue
- Paper plates
- Tea light candles (with metal holders)
- Disposable brush

Dried Flowers

- Enough rosebuds to cover the size of your foam

Tools

- Scissors
- Serrated knife

Note: Read all of the instructions before starting projects.

Instructions

Round candle

1 Paper plate and foam ball. Cut a ½" slice from the top and a 1" slice from the bottom of the ball. Cut a circle from the paper plate to match the bottom of the ball, and glue to secure.

2 Candle. Remove the candle from the metal holder. Mark the foam on the top where the candle will be placed by turning the metal piece upside down and pressing into the foam at the top. Cut out the foam so the tea light will sit 1/2" below the top of the foam. Set the candle and metal holder aside.

3 Glue and rosebuds. Cut the rosebud stems to 1" long. Apply tacky glue to small surfaces of the foam using a disposable brush. Start at the top. Push the bud stems into the foam where the glue is applied. Continue until foam is completely covered. Place candle into metal holder and drop into top of foam.

Pillar candle

1 Floral foam, paper plates, tea lights. Carve the block of floral foam into a pillar shape, approximately 3" thick. Trace the bottom shape of the pillar on a paper plate. Cut out and glue to bottom of foam.

2 Candle. Remove the candle from the metal holder. Mark the foam on the top where the candle will be placed by turning the metal piece upside down and pressing into the foam at the top. Cut out the foam so the tea light will sit 1/2" below the top of the foam. Set the candle and metal holder aside.

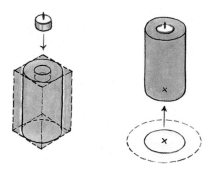

3 Glue and rosebuds. Cut the rosebud stems to 1" long. Apply tacky glue to small surfaces of the foam using a disposable brush. Start at the top. Push the bud stems into the foam where the glue is applied. Continue until foam is completely covered. Place candle into metal holder and drop into top of foam.

European Rendezvous

Materials

- *43" Long X 10" tall, wrought iron wall rack (with three rings for 6" pots)*
- *3 Terra cotta pots 6"*
- *3 Floral foam*
- *Deerfoot moss*
- *Spanish moss*
- *Floral pins*

Silk greens

- *1 Bush piggy back*
- *1 Bush wandering Jew*
- *1 Bush springerii fern (silk or preserved)*
- *1 (Green) cabbage*
- *5-6 Lichen twig branches*

Tools

- *Serrated knife to cut foam.*
- *Hot or low melt glue gun/glue sticks*

Secret: To Distress pots before adding plants, spray with hunter green paint. Allow to dry. Then, dab steel wool into gold paint and rub onto surface.

Set the pots on a shelf, or intermingle them with real house plants in a window greenhouse or an inside garden.

Instructions

1 Floral foam and Spanish moss. Cut foam to fit snugly in all three pots. Glue to bottom to secure. Cover foam with moss, and secure with floral pins.

2 Cabbage, mosses and piggy back bush. Insert bush in back and cabbage in front of one pot. Wrap Spanish moss around trailing vines. Glue deerfoot moss into vines.

3 Springerii fern, deer foot moss, twig branches. Insert fern into second pot. Wind fern around twig branches. Glue deer moss into branches and vines.

4 Wandering Jew and Spanish moss. Insert wandering Jew in front of pot with vines trailing. Add Spanish moss to vines.

Suggested substitutions:
Large ivy for piggyback
Purple passion for wandering Jew
Boston fern for springerii fern
Coleus for cabbage

WOODLAND FANTASY

Materials

- *16" High, 12" wide unfinished doll's rocking chair*
- *3 Pkgs. sheet moss*
- *Bits and pieces of other kinds of moss*
- *3 Strands raffia*
- *Aleene's tacky glue™*
- *Disposable brush*
- *Paper plate*

Silk Flowers

- *14 Stems (assorted colors) pansies*
- *1 Stem dusty miller*
- *2 Stems (white) wild mini daisies*
- *6 Eucalyptus leaves*

Tools

- *Hot or low melt glue gun*
- *Scissors*

Suggested substitutions:
Morning glories for pansies
Ivy for dusty miller
Field flowers for mini dasies
Begonia leaves for eucalyptus

Instructions

1 Chair, moss. Pour tacky glue onto paper plate. Apply liberally to chair in sections with brush. Press moss into glued areas until chair is completely covered.

2 Dried materials and raffia. Wrap raffia around back, arms and legs, and tie bows to secure. Glue flowers and leaves on chair.

Secret: A worn out teddy bear would suit this chair nicely. Spritz the moss with water from time to time to renew and freshen.

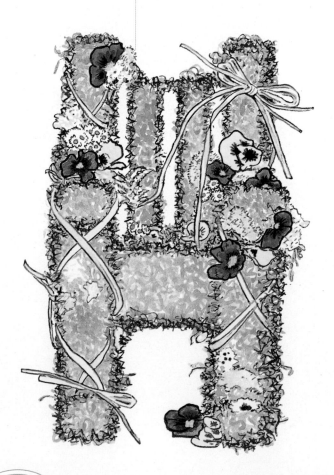

Victorian Heart Wreath

Materials

- Sheet moss
- Forest lichen
- Deerfoot moss
- Aleene's tacky glue™
- Disposable brush
- 12 Strands raffia

Dried Flowers

- 4 Stems pansy blooms
- 1 Stem (purple) larkspur
- 6 Stems globe amaranth
- 2 Stems Australian daisies (white)

Note: Any assortment of dried flowers may be substituted.

Tools

- Scissors
- Hot or low melt glue gun/glue sticks

Instructions

1 Wreath, various mosses. Apply tacky glue liberally to wreath with brush. Press moss into glue until wreath is almost covered. Leave spots of the wreath showing through for texture.

2 Dried materials. Glue dried flowers and other materials, according to photo, with hot glue or tacky glue. Tie raffia bow (see page 20), and glue to dried material.

Secret: Prop it up on a dresser in the bedroom, or a mantlepiece over the fireplace. Hang it low over a shelf, or on a wall filled with greenery. This charming, easy to make heart wreath can go anywhere. Take it to a friend's house, and give it to her or him as a token of affection.

Materials

- 18" straw hat
- 1 Yd. sheer 2" (floral print) ribbon
- 1 Yd. (ivory) tulle ribbon 6" wide
- Floral wire

Dried Flowers

- Small amounts of the following:
  - Plumosus fern,
  - Larkspur (pink)
  - Larkspur (purple)
  - Statice
  - Globe amaranth (pink)
  - 5 Stems (silk) wild roses (burgundy) with buds

Tools

- Hot or low melt glue gun/glue sticks

Suggested substitutions:
Tree fern for plumosus fern
Silk Peruvian lilies for larkspur
Caspia for statice
Allium for globe amaranth
Rununculus for wild roses

Instructions

1 Hat. Trim off *1½"* of brim. Bend rim into crown, and wire to secure.

2 Tulle ribbon. Wrap around crown, and tie into bow.

3 Printed ribbon. Make a loopy bow with 8" tails (see page 21), and glue to top of tulle bow.

4 Wild roses. Glue roses on folded brim. (See photo.)

5 Dried material. Fill in around roses with remaining materials.

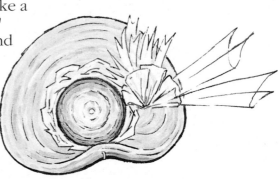

Secret: Glorify any old, battered, straw hat with ribbons and flowers. You can't make a mistake. Hang it on a wall hook, a four poster bed, or throw it on a shelf as a light hearted reminder of pretty things.

GARDEN GATEWAY

Materials

- 3 Lacquered vine trellis (14" X 30" each)
- Florist wire
- 24 Strands natural raffia

Flowers

- 2 Stems (lavender) morning glories
- 2 Stems (white) narcissus
- 6 Stems (in spring colors) tulips
- 2 Stems (yellow) freesias
- 2 Stems small daffodils
- 2 Sprays begonia greenery
- 2 Bunches preserved tree fern
- 6 Lichen twig branches
- 6 Stems (green) onion grass

Tools

- Scissors
- Wire cutters

Suggested substitutions:
Poppies for morning glories
Mini dasies for narcissus
Day lilies for tulips
Statice for freesias
Cosmos for daffodils
Ivy for begonia greenery
Plumosus for tree fern
Ting ting for onion grass

Instructions

1 Trellises. Wire the trellises together making the center one 6" taller than the other two.

2 All the flowers, onion grass and tree fern. Divide the material in half and make two hand bouquets. Use the tulips for height and the morning glories for trailing flowers at the bottom. (Attach to trellis with wire). Curl the ends of the onion grass with scissors.

3 Begonia greenery. Attach sprigs of begonia leaf along the bottom corners and the top arch with floral wire.

4 Raffia. Using sixteen pieces of raffia, make two bows (see page 20). Glue or wire them to the fronts of the bouquets. Weave remaining raffia throughout the trellis.

Project is 42" wide and 36" tall.

Secret:
Hang this charming garden trellis over your bed instead of a headboard.